Chip Carving
Nature

An Artistic
Approach

Craig Vandall Stevens

Text written with and photography by Douglas Congdon-Martin

Schiffer Publishing Ltd

77 Lower Valley Road, Atglen, PA 19310

NO LONGER
PROPERTY OF PPLD

D1243334

118193432

736.4
V224c

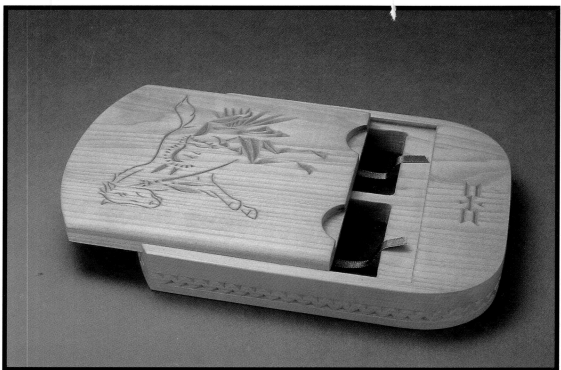

Copyright © 1996 by Craig Vandall Stevens

All rights reserved. No part of this work may be repro-
duced or used in any form or by any means--graphic, elec-
tronic, or mechanical, including photocopying or informa-
tion storage and retrieval systems--without written per-
mission from the copyright holder.

This book is meant only for personal home use and recre-
ation. It is not intended for commercial applications or
manufacturing purposes.

Printed in China

ISBN: 0-7643-0029-6

Book Design by Michael William Potts.

Library of Congress Cataloging-in-Publication Data

Vandall Stevens, Craig
   Chip carving nature : an artistic approach / Craig
Vandall Stevens; text written with and photography by
Douglas Congdon-Martin.
      p.   cm.
   ISBN 0-7643-0029-6 (pbk.)
      1. Wood-carving--Technique. 2. Nature (Aesthetics)
I. Congdon-Martin, Douglas. II. Title.
TT199.7.V35   1996
736'.4--dc20   96-19276
                                                  CIP

PROPERTY OF
PIKES PEAK LIBRARY DISTRICT
P.O. BOX 1579
COLORADO SPRINGS CO 80901

Published by Schiffer Publishing, Ltd.
77 Lower Valley Road
Atglen, PA 19310
Phone: (610) 593-1777
Fax: (610) 593-2002

Please write for a free catalog.
This book may be purchased from the publisher.
Please include $2.95 for shipping.
Try your bookstore first.

We are interested in hearing from
authors with book ideas on related subjects.

CONTENTS

Dedication

This book is dedicated to my niece and fellow woodworker Carly, who at age 6 reminds me of the importance of making something simply for the joy of doing so.

Acknowledgments

I would like to express my appreciation for Caroline who shares this adventure with a sense of humor, endless support, and a lighthearted spirit. She will surely one day be sainted. I would like to thank my mother, Patricia Stevens-Sahli, for encouraging my imagination and enthusiastically displaying my "artwork" on the refrigerator all those years. Also Richard, my computer guru, who really thinks I know what a megabyte is. I'd like to express my gratitude to John and Elaine for their understanding and help and for proudly showing off my work at every opportunity. I would also like to thank Nancy Roberts for drawing upon her elegant knowledge of language to try and keep me out of trouble with the grammar police.

I'd like to acknowledge the staff at the College of the Redwoods Fine Woodworking Program, Jim Krenov, Michael Burns, David Welter, and Jim Budlong, who each encouraged my desire to continue refining my style of chip carving and explore the relationship between fine woodworking and chip carving.

Finally, I would like to thank the nice folks at Schiffer Publishing for taking an interest in my work, especially Doug Congdon-Martin for his skills and sense of humor.

INTRODUCTION

Several years ago I saw a simple repeated pattern carved down the legs of a small table. The idea that such a small, subtle detail could add so much interest to the piece of furniture germinated my interest in chip carving. I realized that the carving, which was barely noticeable across the room, had drawn me to look more closely. The idea of inviting someone to explore an object more intimately, whether with a carving, marquetry, or other interesting choices one makes, is an aspect of woodworking that holds a tremendous amount of appeal for me. This is part of what my (furniture making) teacher, Jim Krenov calls the fingerprints of the craftsman

Chip carving has allowed me to put into use a lifelong interest in drawing and sketching. I feel that this has benefitted my carving. Likewise, the desire to carve interesting designs has probably enhanced my ability to draw because the drawing has a purpose. Many of my carving students have expressed hesitancy or intimidation at the idea of working on their own designs, stating an inability to draw as the reason. I encourage the reader as I do my students, to at least give it an occasional try. (You can always hide those first few sketches in the bottom of a drawer or somewhere else never to be found by anyone else!) Like carving, drawing improves with practice and can become a very satisfying aspect of chip carving. If you have little or no experience at drawing but would like to learn more, you might look into cultural arts centers or adult education programs. As you'll see on the following pages, the designs included here are inspired by nature.

Oriental brush painting, too, is inspired by nature, and has been a source of inspiration for me. The master brush painters of Japan and China are able to capture the grace of nature in their paintings with a minimum of brushstrokes, often allowing the eye of the viewer to "complete" the image or suggestion of movement in the work.

The style I demonstrate here is an effort to create an image using carved shapes and patterns rather than outlining the subject. I hope to convey a degree of the brush painter's sensitivity through the flow and movement of these carved shapes, imitating the simple but graceful patterns of the natural world. The initial drawing creates the foundation of each carving. After transferring the sketch to the wood, the actual carving begins. Because this approach to design requires the blending of two disciplines, I often find that the knife leads me in a direction different from my original drawing. In the process of working within this suggestive style, I've come to view chip carving as an opportunity to "compose" directly from the point of the knife, allowing the combined effort of hand, eye, and knife to create the carved image.

In this book I will discuss the technique of chip carving including the tools and their care, sharpening and wood selection, as well as design and transferring the drawing to the wood. I'll take a project from the artwork, through the carving and finishing of the work.

I wish you luck in exploring this style of chip carving and hope you enjoy the adventure.

Suggestions

1. Make an effort to keep the elbow of your carving arm relaxed and at your side. This allows more strength and control to be directed to the knife, making the carving safer, more accurate, and less tiresome. Besides looking funny, your elbow sticking out means you're not fully using the muscles of your arm and shoulder.

2. Work on your lap when possible. The distance to your lap is just right to help keep your elbow at your side. If you prefer to work at a bench, position yourself (standing or seated) so that your elbow is relaxed and near your body.

3. When working on a small piece, use a larger lap size piece of wood below the workpiece to give additional support and lessen the chance of slipping and cutting yourself.

4. Secure your workpiece when using harder woods or larger pieces.

5. Wear a bandaid on the thumb of your carving hand to prevent your thumbnail from scratching or damaging the work surface.

6. Use an index card to cover delicate, intricately carved area's as you near completion. The card is easily repositioned for each cut to protect what you've already carved.

7. The hand *holding* the workpiece is most likely to be cut in case of a slip. Develop the habit of holding the work above the knife so that it's not in the path of the blade.

What wood should I use?

I consider four things when I choose woods.

1. Hardness: The wood has to be soft enough that it can be carved using only the strength of your hand, but not so soft that it crushes under the cutting edge of the knife.

2. Color: Lighter colored woods show off the contrast between shadow and light better than darker woods.

3. Close, fine grain: Close grained, finely textured woods like basswood, hold detail very well. The result is a nice, crisp look to the carving.

4. Grain Pattern: Some woods, like butternut, have distinct grain patterns. The grain is often beautiful, but it can compete with the carving for attention. More subtle grain patterns as in basswood and pear help the carving stand out.

I would suggest using basswood for chip carving, especially when just starting out. It meets all four of the above considerations, is readily available, and is a pleasure to use.

I must admit that I don't always follow these guidelines. For instance, my favorite wood to use in chip carving is Swiss pear, but it is quite hard and I've had to build up the hand strength to carve it. Since I often use chip carving to decorate the furniture I make, I sacrifice ease of carving for the beauty and strength a wood like pear brings to the piece.

Suggested Woods
  Basswood
  Poplar
  White Pine
  Butternut
  Mahogany
  Walnut

Uncommon woods
  European (Swiss) Pear
  Sugar Pine
  Alaskan Yellow Cedar
  Port Orford Cedar
  Nutmeg
  Buckeye

A word about **Lesser Known Species**. Over the past few years many new woods have become available to woodworkers and carvers. Some of these woods are suitable for chip carving and are certainly worth exploring. Many of these are ecologically harvested species from well-managed sources and available through specialized suppliers. Two lesser known species that offer chip carving possibilities are:

Narra, a golden-brown wood from Papua New Guinea.

Chokte kok, a deep red wood that mellows to a red-brown from the Yucatan Peninsula.

FINISHES

After careful clean-up of the carving apply a finish to protect the wood and add richness to the grain. I prefer a clear low-gloss or matte finish and have had success using shellac or polyurethane varnish. Both are available in a spray. Sand or use 0000 steel wool between coats. I avoid finishes that tend to yellow bass wood, such as oil. Experiment on some carved scraps before applying a finish to your completed work.

SHARPENING

The carving knife (Number one) is the workhorse of chip carving and requires the most preparation. The two goals in sharpening are to keep a perfectly straight cutting edge and to reduce the angle of the bevel. This takes metal off the shoulder behind the cutting edge, reducing drag in the wood and increasing the maneuverability of the knife as you carve.

I use two, small ceramic sharpening stones for my carving knives. The darker is a medium , fast cutting grit and the white stone is considered super fine. Because they are made from a very hard, synthetic material, they stay perfectly flat. Other stones are usually softer and begin to dish-out with use. The problem is that the shape of the stone is transferred to the cutting edge of the knife, so a dished-out sharpening surface gives you a curved cutting edge.

Ceramic stones need no lubricant, making them cleaner and very portable. They are good, lifetime tools that I highly recommend.

Sharpening time for me is a creative time which allows me to begin to focus my attention on my carving. Not only does it prepare the knives for use, it also sharpens my mind and prepares me for the work ahead.

The first sharpening of the knife will be time consuming. People in my carving class often spend their entire first evening preparing their knife. The initial sharpening is on the medium stone. The ideal angle is 10 degrees. Noted chip carver Wayne Barton has given the best suggestion for determining that angle. Simple lay a dime under the back edge of the blade and try to consistently sharpen at that angle.

Carving knife held on the sharpening stone with the back edge raised to a 10 degree angle (approximately the thickness of a dime).

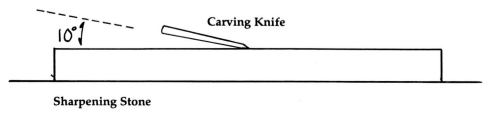

Carving Knife

10°

Sharpening Stone

The bevel of a new knife (**left**) has a steep angle with thick shoulders just behind the cutting edge. Correctly sharpened (**right**), the angle has been reduced to about 10 degrees and the shoulder is less prominent.

The idea of creating a perfectly sharp edge can be demonstrated by viewing each of the two sharpening angles as a plane. The two planes must cross precisely at the cutting edge to create a burr. As the burr is reduced by honing, a perfectly sharp cutting edge emerges that is straight and reflects no light. A common mistake is to stop sharpening before the two angles cross, resulting in a tiny flat area along the cutting edge.

After a number of strokes on one side, flip the blade over to do the other side. Again, you want to keep the ten degree angle. Stop occasionally mid-stroke and mentally check for the dime's thickness. Repeat the process again and again, slowly eliminating the factory shoulder. The knife is sharp when the planes of the two sides of the blade intersect.

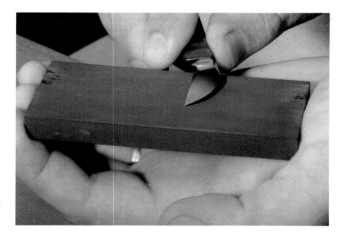

Hold the stone in your hand or on a bench and imagine the dime thickness. Rub the blade back and forth on the stone perpendicular to the cutting edge, using medium pressure. When holding the stone in my hand I keep my fingers below the surface of the stone for safety. Focus your attention and pressure on the middle of the cutting edge. If I apply more pressure at the point it puts a slight curve in the cutting edge or rounds the point.

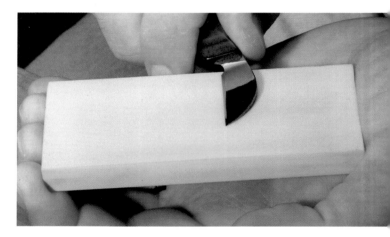

After some time you will begin to engage the cutting edge on the stone creating a burr. It can be felt with the finger. With continued sharpening you will begin to reduce the burr, until finally it is so thin it breaks away. At that point it is time to switch to the super fine white stone. The white stone hones the sharpened edge, creating a mirror finish on the cutting surface. By polishing the surface, You allow the blade to move smoothly through the wood, reducing the friction and giving you a fluid, easy flow through the wood. Use lighter pressure on the white stone.

A microscopic burr is created during sharpening, and the sharpening is complete when the burr is eliminated. This burr is so small that it is difficult to feel. To find it I hold the blade under direct light and look at the cutting edge from the spine. If there is a burr it will reflect a glint of light in a fine line, and I know I need to sharpen a little more.

A final check for sharpness involves look straight down on the blade and turning it in the light. If the planes intersect completely, there will be no reflecting of light on the edge of the blade. If they are slightly off, I will see a glint of light.

When to touch up an edge depends on many factors, including the type of wood you are carving. It is not unusual to have to hone a knife soon after it is sharpened. It seems that the more a knife is sharpened the longer it holds its edge. When the knife gets dull, you should be able to get a fresh edge using only the super fine white stone. After many honings you may wish to use the medium stone again to create a new edge.

The bevel of the stab knife is roughly 30 degrees. It is correct as it comes from the factory and the sharpening we do is simply to polish the bevel. Start with the medium stone until you create a fine burr and then work it away.

Finish with the white stone.

HAND POSITIONS

The basic blade angle is about 65 degrees, although I vary this at the beginning and end of a cut. The tendency of new carvers is to stand the knife up too much, carving too deeply.

Having used many knives, the ones I've come to prefer are Wayne Barton's, primarily because the length and angle of the blade allows my hand to be close to the work.

The basic motion is to plunge into the wood and follow the line with the cutting edge. At the same time you need to visualize the location of the point of the knife.

There are two hand positions with the carving knife. The primary grip forms a tripod between the knife, the thumb, and the first joint of the forefinger. This gives stability and control to the carving action. I try to keep my thumb and forefinger in contact with the knife handle at all times.

In the second position the first joint of the forefinger rides on the wood, but the knife is rotated so the thumb is putting pressure on the spine. The action is to plunge away from you. The angle of the knife is the same as in the first position. This position is helpful in shapes like triangles and for cleaning up some wood fibers that may have not been cut away.

The stab knife is held as though you were going to stab the work piece.

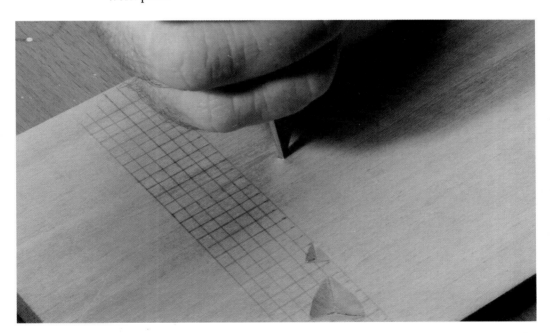

By pressing it into the wood, it severs the fibers...

and creates an indentation. This can be lengthened and changes by rocking the blade.

CARVING BASICS

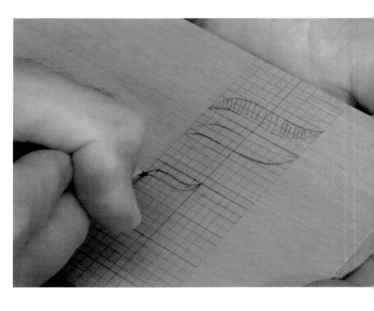

Draw some s-shapes of various sizes using the grid.

A word about safety.

Sharp knives go a long way towards preventing injuries because less pressure is required to manipulate the knife. It is also important to be aware of what you are doing, especially concerning the hand that is holding the work piece. Keep it out of the path of the knife. If you are working on your lap, be especially careful near the edge of the work piece. When working on a small carving on your lap, use a larger piece of wood below the carving to protect your legs.

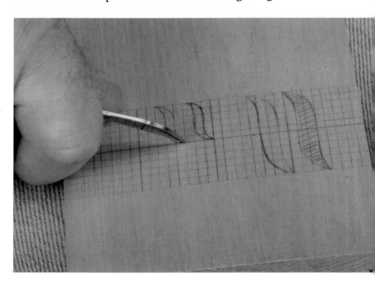

Start with a smaller s-shape. Place the knife in the corner, almost straight up.

To learn the basic strokes I create a grid on a 4" x 12" board of basswood. Basswood is a good wood for beginners. It is easy to carve, available and inexpensive. The grid lines are 1/8" apart.

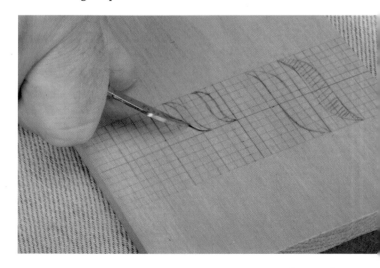

Follow the line, leaning the knife over to about 65 degrees in the middle of the cut.

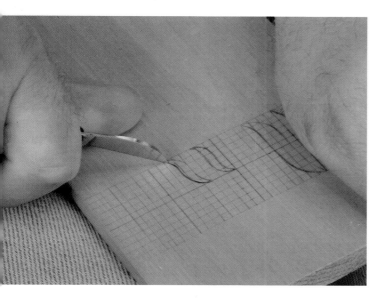

At the end of the cut rotate your wrist so the knife is nearly vertical again.

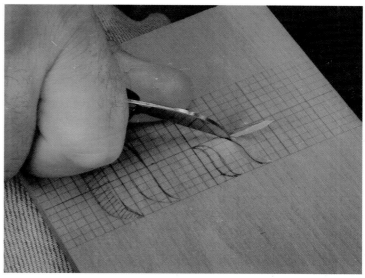

End with the blade vertical. With practice this should free the flowing wedge in the middle...

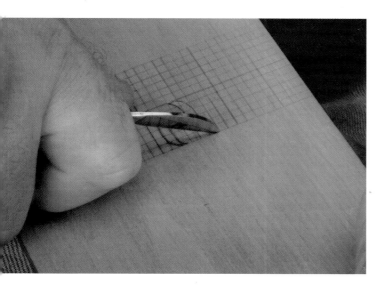

Turn the board around to do the other side. The process is the same. Start at the corner with your knife vertical.

and leave you with this result.

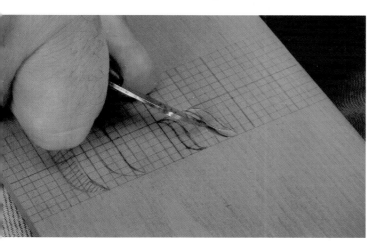

Lean it over as you come down the side.

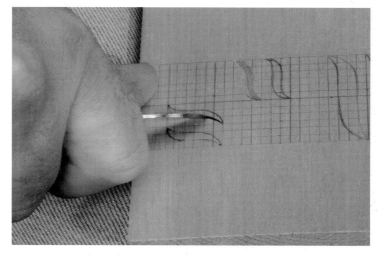

Next draw the mirror image of the s-shape, with the curves going in the opposite direction.

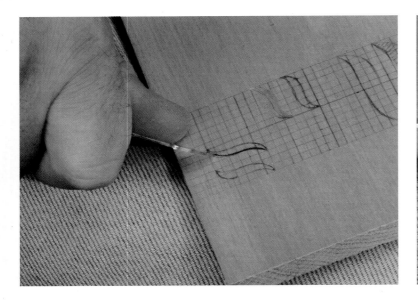

Again start in the corner, but cut the concave curve first. Use a good deal of pressure on this first cut carrying it to the end.

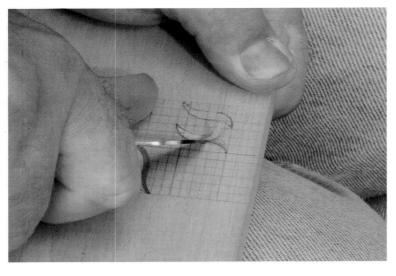

Turn the board and repeat the cut on the other side of the figure. Start in the corner but use only enough pressure to take out the chip, not to undercut the first cut.

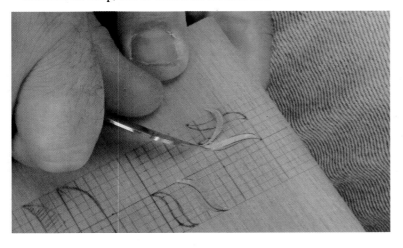

End with the knife blade vertical.

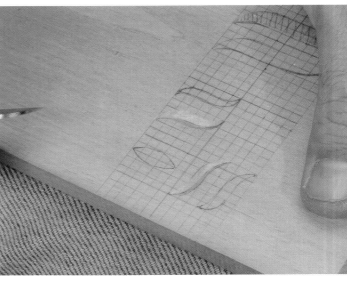

The next practice shape is a pointed oval.

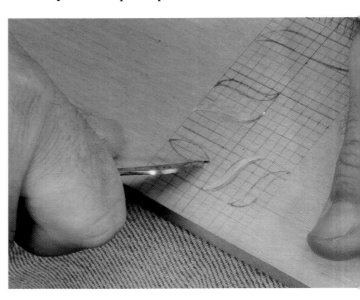

Start at the corner with the knife vertical and shallow.

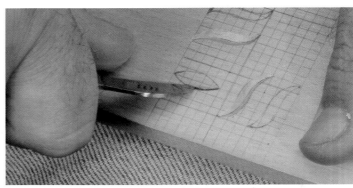

Here you make the transition from cutting with the grain to cutting against the grain. As the blade becomes parallel to the direction of the grain, you must "slip the blade." This is done by sliding the blade slightly out of the cut while continuing your forward progress, severing the wood fibers and preventing the blade from the taking off with the grain.

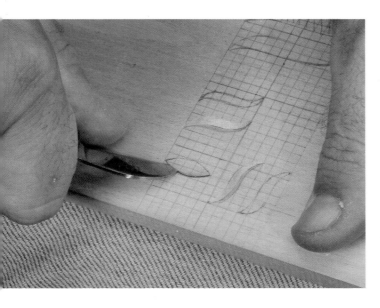

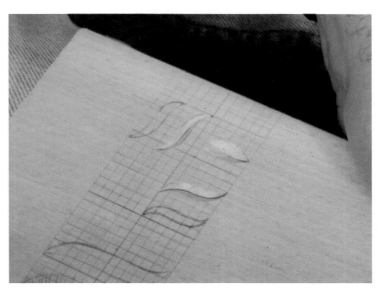

As you continue you can push the knife more deeply into the grain. This may leave some fibers in the trough of the cut, but these are easily cleaned out later if necessary.

The result.

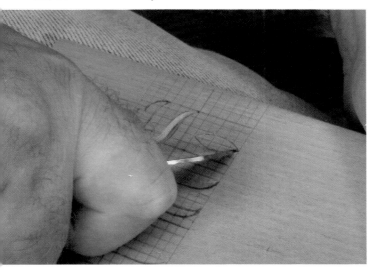

Repeat the process on the other side, starting at the corner...

When you are comfortable with the smaller figures, move to the larger. The technique is the same, but it requires more hand strength. Because you need so much more pressure, be sure the thumb of your holding hand is out of the way in case the knife slips.

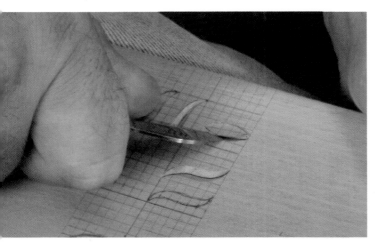

and slipping the blade at the turn. Here the grain is even more likely to tear because it has lost its support in the previous cut.

Next practice straight and curved lines. The two straight lines are of different thicknesses.

Start at the end. I find it works best if I focus my attention just in front of the blade. When I can do this I always end up with a straighter, more even line.

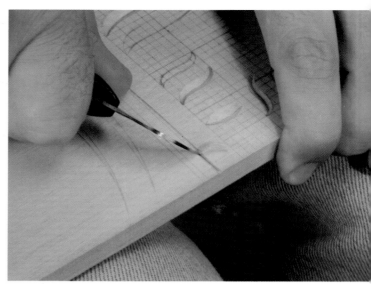

Turn the work and cut the other side of the line. This requires much less pressure because it is simply a relieving cut. Too much pressure and you undercut the first cut.

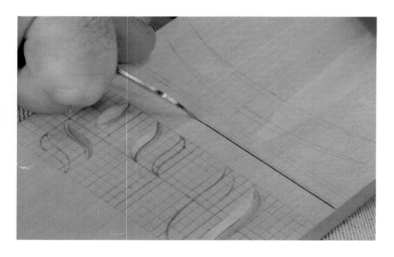

Maintain even pressure through the cut.

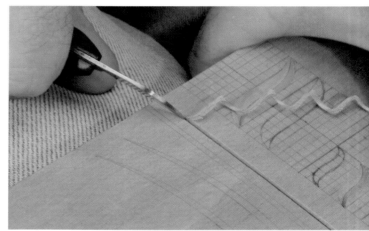

Continue through the line and end it in the same way.

As you approach the end of the cut, your hand leaves the board, making it more difficult to maintain the cutting position. Use your leg or work surface as an extension of the board. At the very end of the cut, before your knife leaves the board, stop and pivot it down into the wood.

The curved line is cut with the same technique. Focus your attention in front of the blade and keep an even pace and pressure.

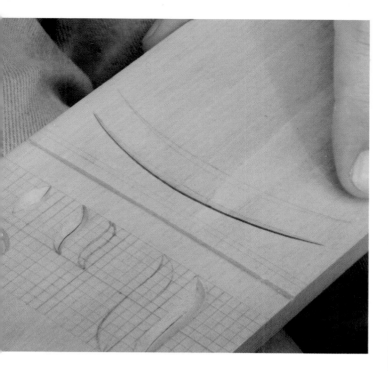

One side of the cut finished. At the ends the blade is more vertical and uses very little pressure.

The concave side is done in the same way, starting shallow and more vertical at the end...

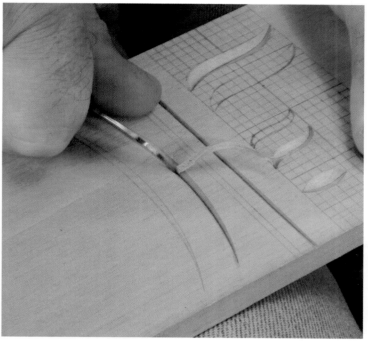

leaning the blade over and going deeper in the middle...

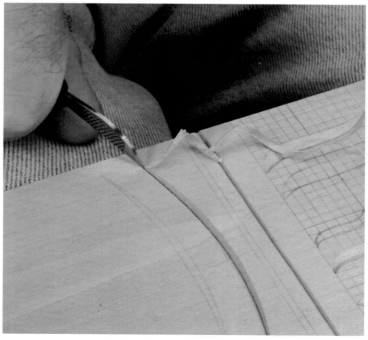

and finishing with the blade vertical and shallow.

CARVING THE GIRAFFE

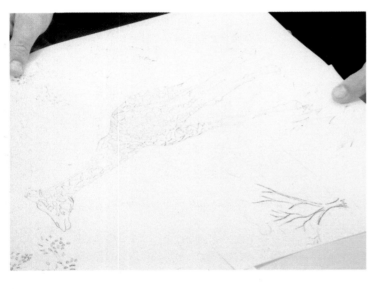

The pattern needs to enlarged 200% to reach its original size. You will need to do this in sections on a copy machine, then tape them together.

Transfer the pattern to the board. I am using a basswood board that is 22" x 14". It is planed flat and sanded with 400 grit paper. I sand carefully now because sanding after the carving tends to soften the crisp, sharp edges of the carving. Transfer the pattern by placing a piece of graphite paper, graphite side down, between the tracing and the board and going over the lines. I use a mechanical pencil with 0.5mm lead. I use a lead softness of B so I don't have to push too hard to transfer the line. It is important to tape down one edge of the tracing to keep it in position on the board.

Copy the pattern onto tracing paper.

We'll begin by outlining the head of the giraffe. Start with the lower jaw.

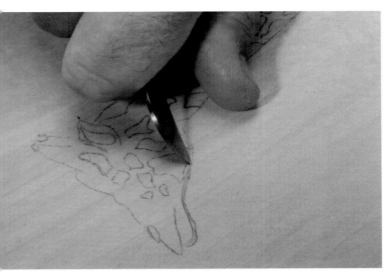

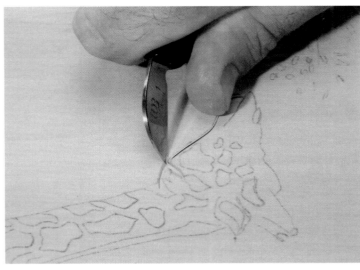

Make a smooth cut following the curve of the jaw line...

swelling the cut at the back of the jaw...

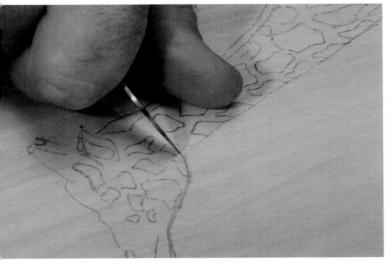

back to the neck.

narrowing it as the line becomes concave...

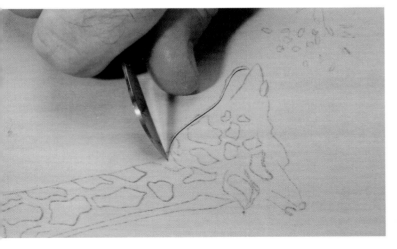

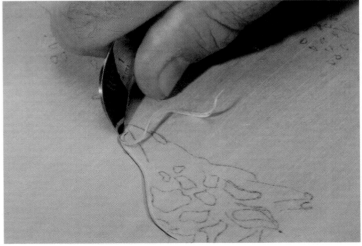

The return cut defines the line. I don't want it to be perfectly parallel with the first cut. Some widening or narrowing of the line gives dimensionality to the work. I widen the line at places where there would be more shadow and depth, and narrow it where there would be less. Begin the return at the neck...

and swelling again at the front of the jaw. At this tight curve it is easier to change the position of the wood than to change your hand position.

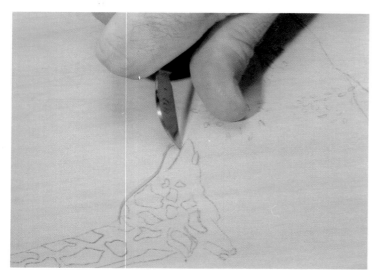

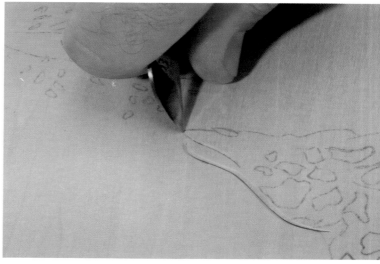

Start the cut of the mouth. You want the first cut of a line to be away from previous cuts so you don't create breakage. Starting at the back keeps the tip of the knife pointed away from the lower jaw cut.

Begin the next cut where the last ended.

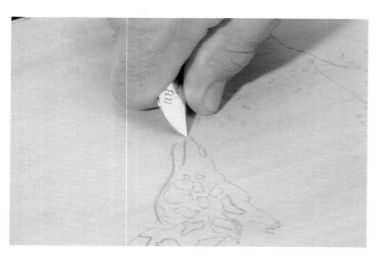

At the upper lip, I choke up on the knife for control, and go far enough to begin the turn toward the nose.

Cut up to the nostril.

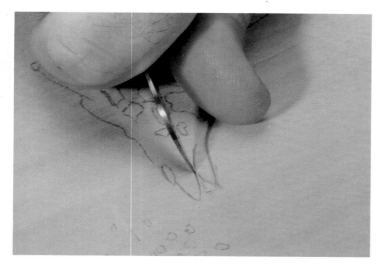

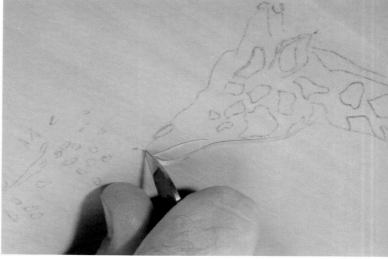

Cut the return.

Cut the return.

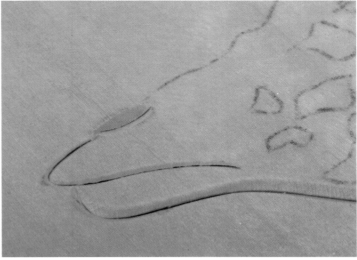

The nostril is a chip cut rather than a line. Start on the bottom so you are working with the point of your knife away from the previous cut.

for this result.

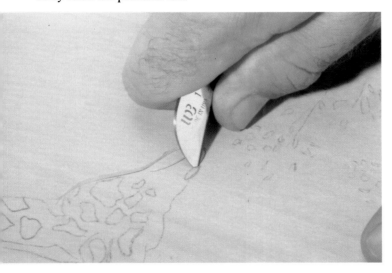

Continue to the front.

Continue carving the outline of the face.

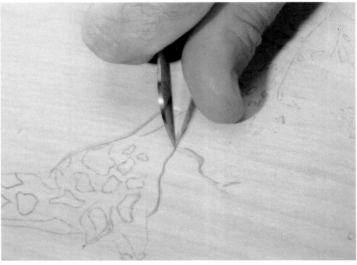

Carve back along the top line...

Cut the return, making the line wider at the top of the head.

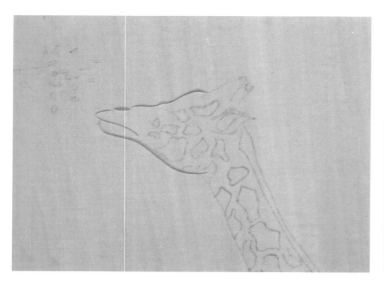

Progress. Because the bottom line of the head is in shadow and the top in the sunlight, I've made the lines a little wider along the bottom.

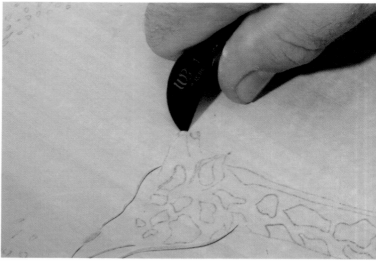

When you reach the knob of the horn, stand the knife up a little to begin the curve. This reduces the amount of metal in the wood without changing the depth of the cut, making it easier to make the turn.

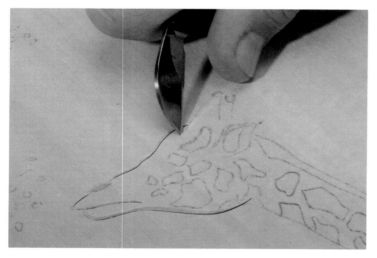

Start the line of the horn below the line of the forehead. This overlap gives perspective to the work, making it look as though the horn is closer to the viewer.

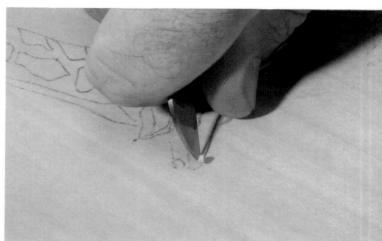

Choke up on the knife, raise the blade, and cut the bottom line of the knob.

Continue up the horn.

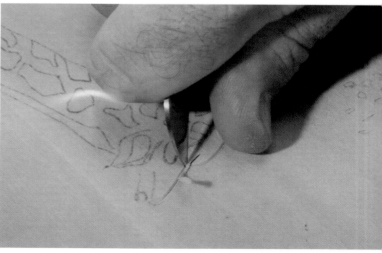

Continue with the return cut of the horn line.

Carry the line of the back of the horn up to the knob, but stop before cutting into the knob. The little ridge left will bring out the knob.

On the other horn, the front line disappears behind the forward horn. This is suggested with a teardrop shape cut for the knob. Start at the point of the cut and choke up on the knife to raise the angle of the blade.

At the end of this line make a slight turn...

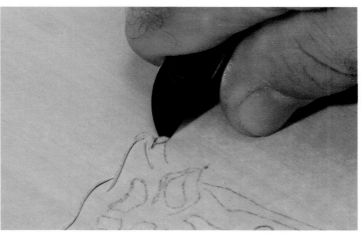

Make a curving cut to the end of the knob...

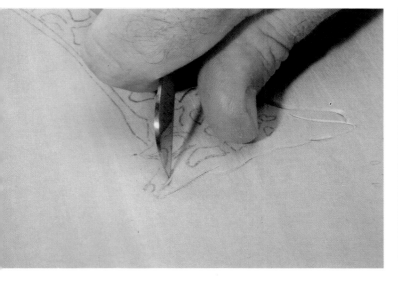

then return on the other side of the line.

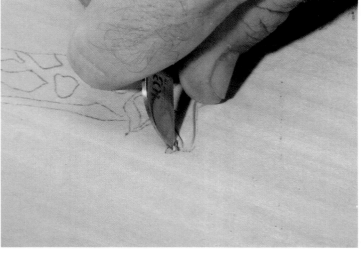

then turn the wood and make a relieving cut in the lower line of the knob down to the point.

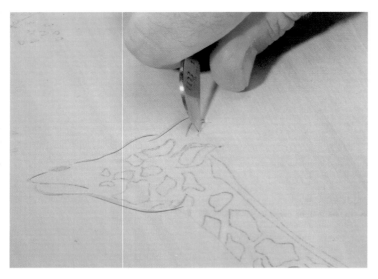

To finish the horn cut the back line...

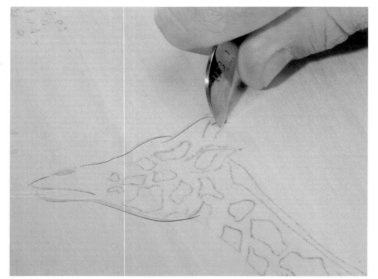

stop just shy of the knob.

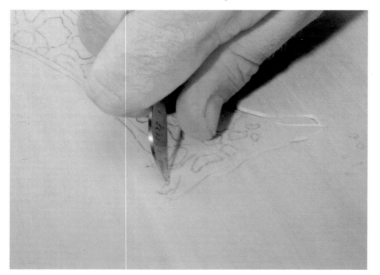

Make the return.

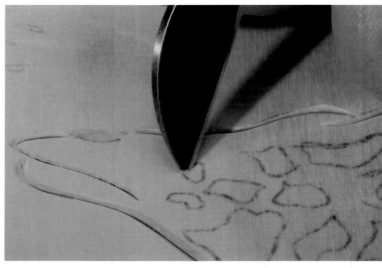

The spots are basically three or four sided shapes with irregular sides. Sometimes one side will blend into the other without a definite stopping or starting point. We'll start with this three sided spot. Plunge the knife in...

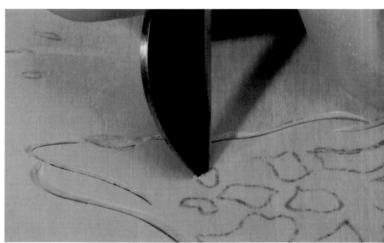

and follow the curve of the side by rotating the knife.

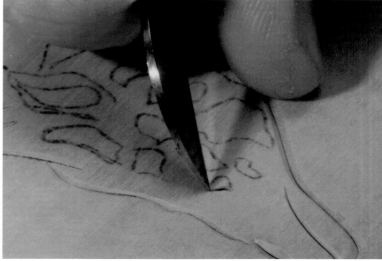

Begin the second cut where the first cut left off...

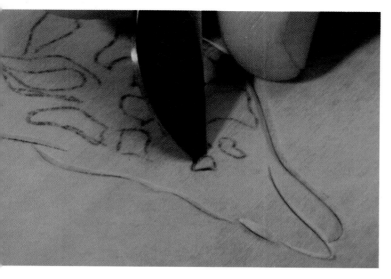

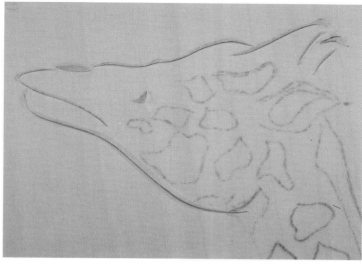

and curve the cut the opposite way.

The result.

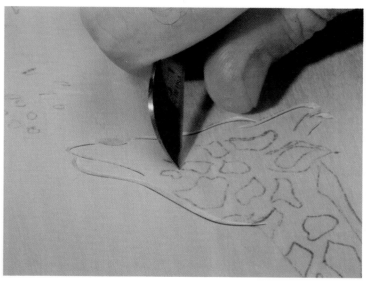

Again begin where you left off, choke up on the blade as you plunge it in...

This larger spot has a nice curve on the upper line. The technique is the same. Plunge in...

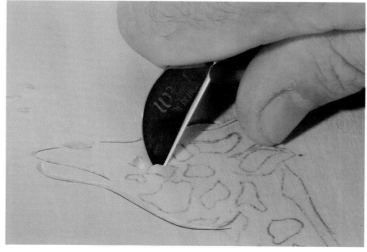

and finish the cut.

and follow the curve by rotating the knife.

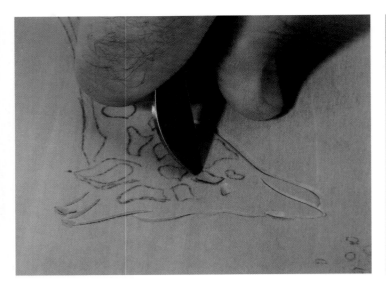

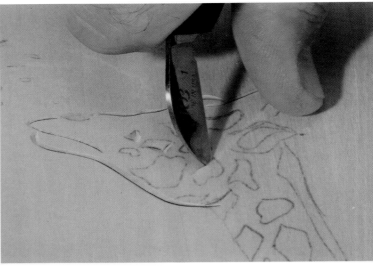

Begin the second side where you finished the first. At the end of this cut pull your knife out slightly. This allows you to turn the knife enough to begin the curve of the last side.

and stand the blade up at the end of the cut.

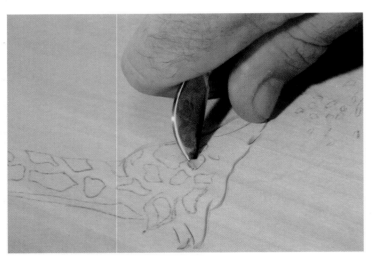

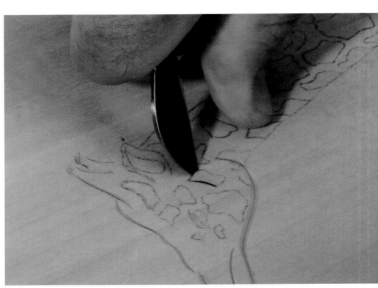

The final side has a convex curve to finish the spot.

Cut the second side in the same way.

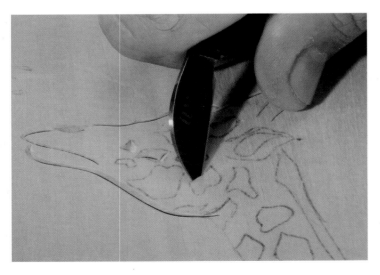

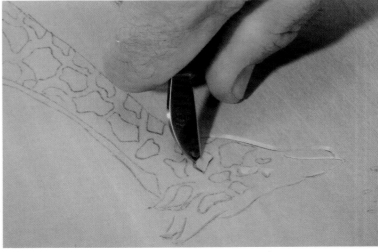

The four-sided spot is done in a similar way. Plunge in, follow the curve...

This double curved third line requires a little more care. Plunge in...

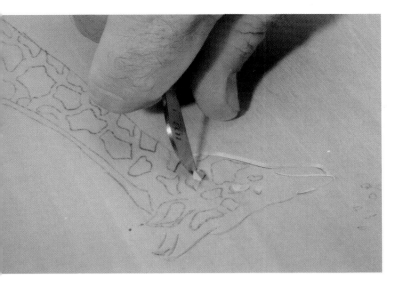

and follow the curves.

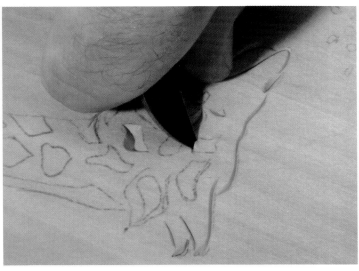

The eye is a two-sided cut with some sharp turns in it. I start on the bottom because I have already cut out a spot below the eye. Choking up for maneuverability, plunge in...

Cut the fourth side...

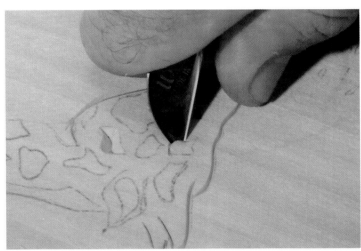

and follow the curve.

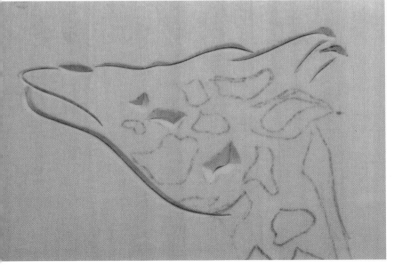

and the spot is formed.

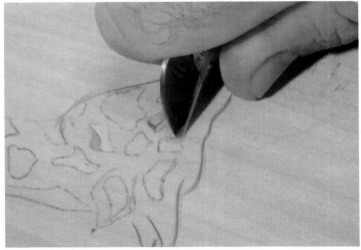

At the end of the cut, pull the knife out and rotate it at the same time.

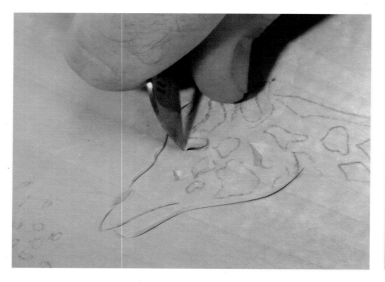

Start at the front corner, still choked up on the knife, and plunge in with a shallow cut...

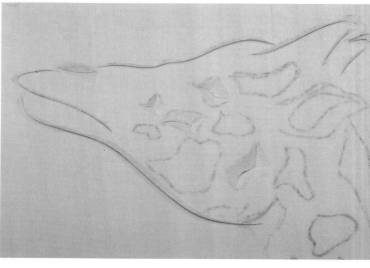

The finished eye.

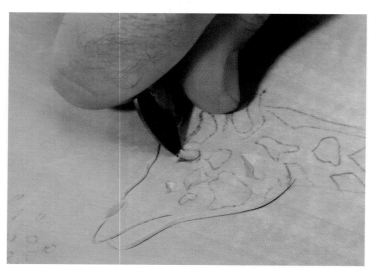

Go deep to the first curve then pull the blade out to make a tight turn.

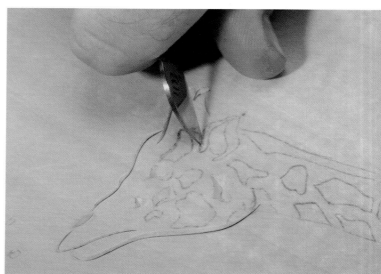

The ear is basically two two-sided cuts. The first, at the front of the ear starts at the base...

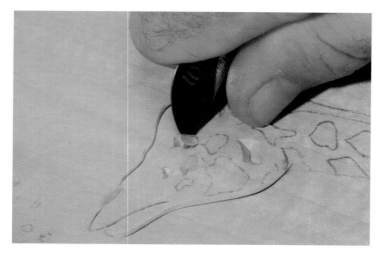

Go deep again to the back corner.

and goes out to the tip.

Make a return cut.

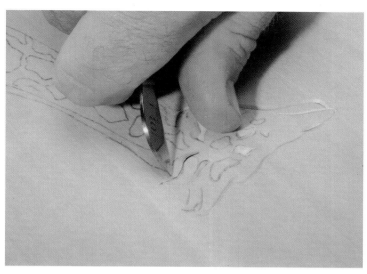

Begin the return very shallowly...

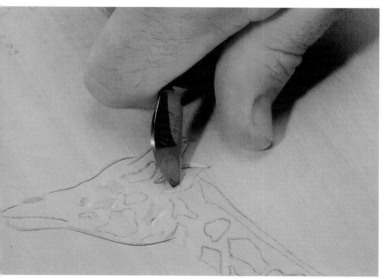

The second cut is the trailing side of the ear. Cut with the knife pointed away from the previous cut, starting at the base and working out.

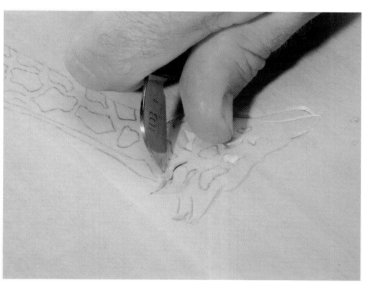

get deeper at the middle...

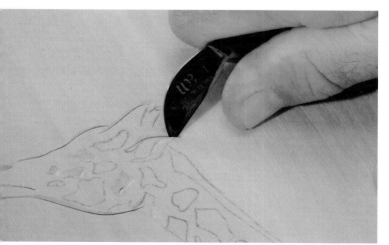

At the end of the cut you want to leave a ridge with the first cut.

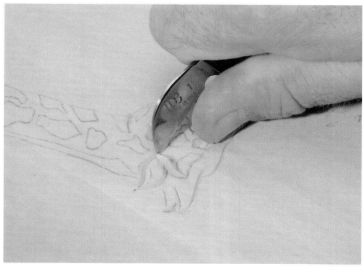

and finish shallowly.

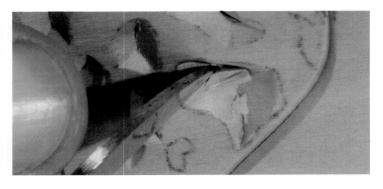

Where there is an outline, such as here on the face, you need to leave a ridge between the spot and the outline.

There is no outline around the neck and body. Instead the shape is suggested by the spots and the mane.

With the irregular shapes of the giraffe spots it is more than likely that you will leave some fibers in the cut. When it happens you can clean the cut by carefully laying the knife so it follows the plane of the original cut, and gently pushing it deeper to sever the fibers.

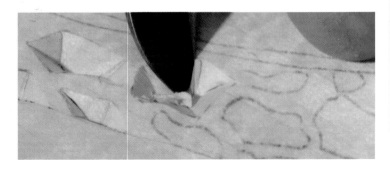

Continue around the cut, wherever you see fibers uncut...

until the cut is clean. If your angle is wrong or you cut too deeply, you may leave the bottom of the cut looking sloppy. Careful, accurate cuts will lead to nice crisp results.

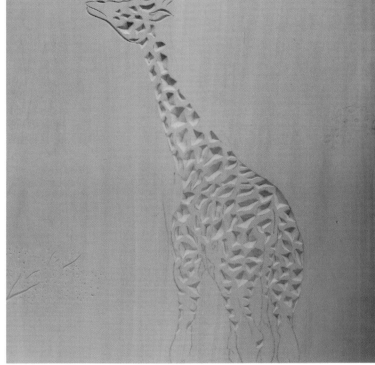

Continue down the body with the spots.

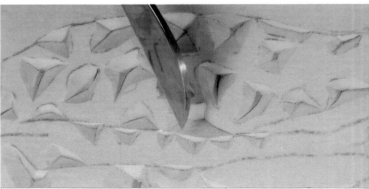

There are places where the spots define a portion of the body, allowing me to keep the use of lines to a minimum. Here at the tail, the ridge between the spots of the tail and the adjacent spots of the haunches, creates the line of the tail.

This spot at the top of the hind leg acts in the same way. The long curved cut follows the line of the leg.

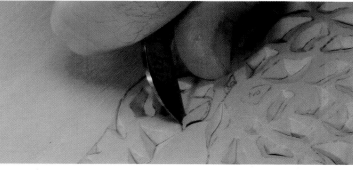

The third cut returns to the start. Slip the blade as you run into the change in grain direction.

The return is a single cut, helping this spot suggest the graceful curve of the leg.

To clean up this spot, I switch my knife position and carefully cut the fibers that are holding.

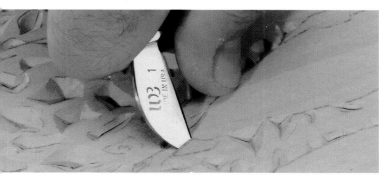

The spot at the top of the front leg completes the shape of the leg for the viewer's eye. Its outside line starts at the top with the first cut.

This small spot is on the front leg. The right side defines the edge of the back leg, with the spot appearing to be hidden behind it. The small size of the spot also adds to the suggestion of distance. This is a three sided cut, starting down the side against the back leg.

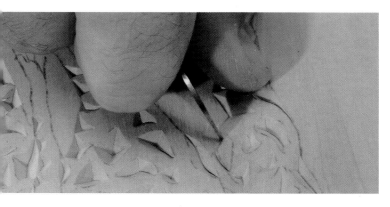

The second cut comes down the edge of the leg.

The second cut is one stroke but has a quick turn in it, accomplished by standing the knife up straight and pivoting.

Go deep again to finish the second cut.

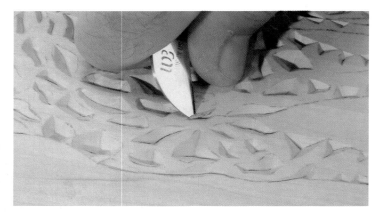

The third cut completes the spot and should lift the chip.

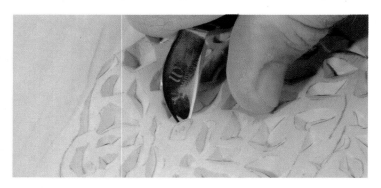

The last drawn spot is a three sided cut. I start on the long curved side so I carve away from a previously carved spot. Slip the knife to make the curve.

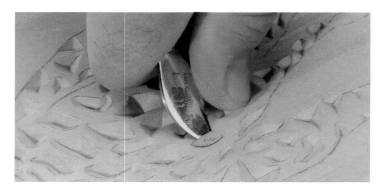

Carve the second side...

and the third. While this was the last drawn spot, as you examine the piece you may decide another spot or two are needed to define the contour of the animal.

I need to add a small spot on the front edge of the back leg to more clearly define its shape.

It is opposite the small spot we just carved on the front leg but shifted slightly higher. The ridge left between the adjacent sides will suggest the line of the haunch to the viewer.

Start with the adjacent side, cutting away from the previous cut and forming a ridge. Because this spot is on the contour of the haunch and we are seeing only its edge, it appears narrow.

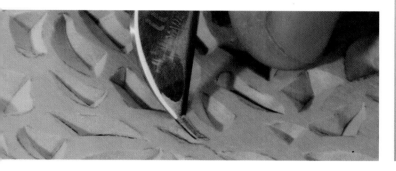

Cut the short side with a plunge cut.

Because of the direction of the grain, it will be easier to change to the second knife position to cut the other long side.

A final plunge cut on the other short side finishes the spot.

I've broken the mane into four segments to give it movement and make it less imposing on the eye.

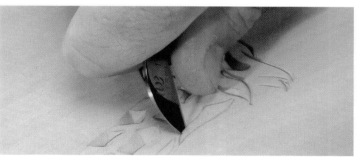

The top segment has three cuts to follow the contour of the back of the head. Start shallow and go deep standing the knife up at the end of the cut.

The second cut plunges in where the first left off...

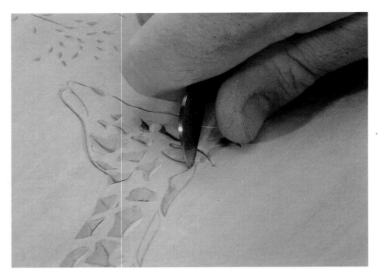

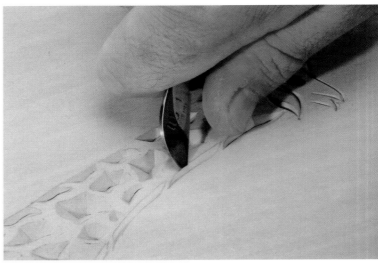

The blade is slipped to make the end of the cut shallow.

The segments should be irregular as are the spots. Try to vary the shapes and the spaces between the segments. The direction of the cut should start up the mane segment, working away from the previous carved spots.

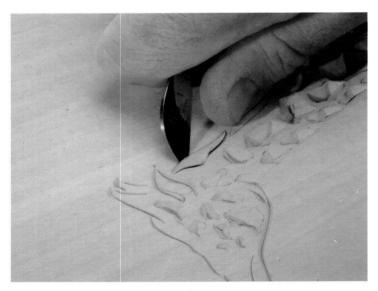

The final cut starts shallow, goes deep in the middle...

Cut back on the other side.

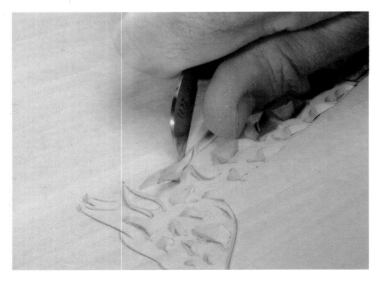

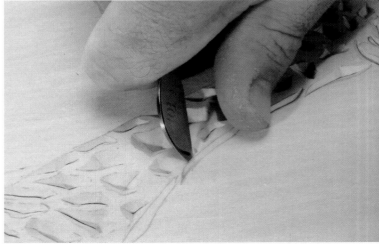

and ends shallow.

This third segment is a little longer and not quite as flowing as the second. Start shallow on the first cut away from the neck...

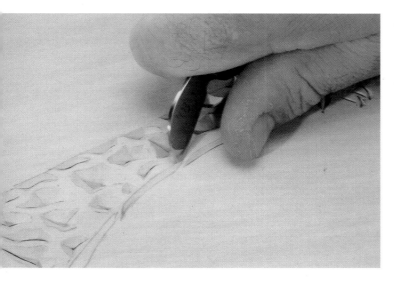

go deep and end shallow.

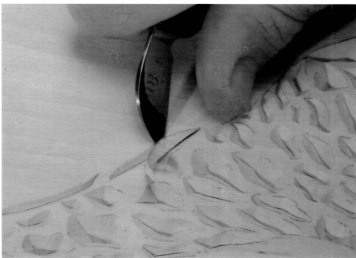

Complete the segment.

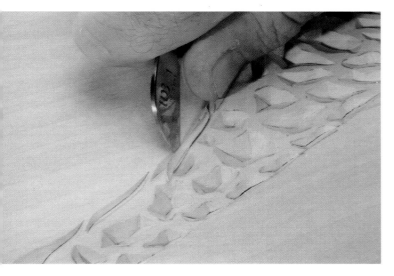

Cut the other side in the same way.

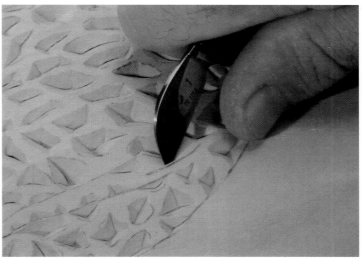

The high point of the upper tail is suggested with a line. This is a simple two-cut line. Cut up...

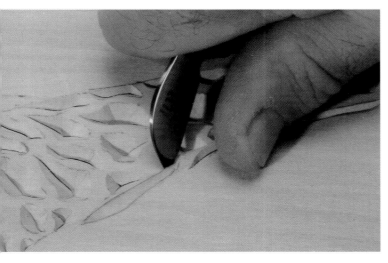

The final segment of the mane is more irregular. Cut away from the neck. This cut comes close to the spots and will form a ridge with at least one of them.

and make the return.

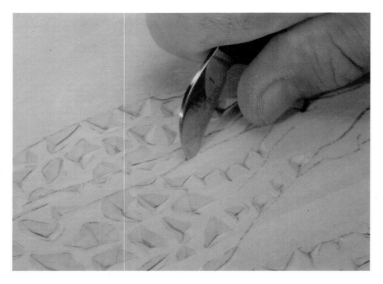

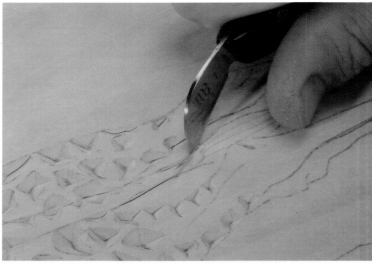

The edge of the lower portion of the tail is also suggested with lines. Cut down one edge...

and make the return to relieve the chip. Neither of these lines should touch anything at the ends. Leave it to the imagination of the viewer to complete the line.

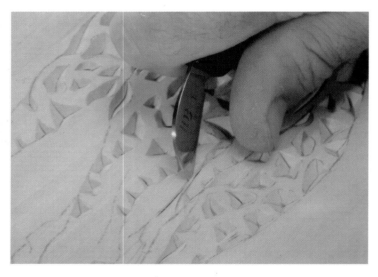

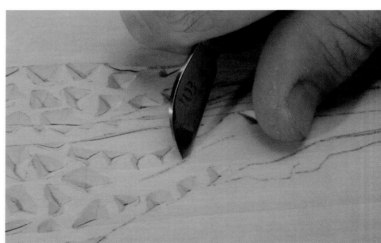

and make the return.

This fine line suggests the tendon of the back leg at the knee. Cut down with a fluid flat s-cut...

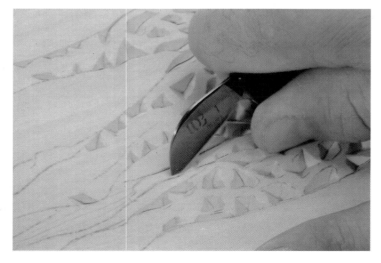

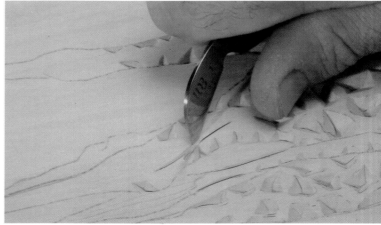

The other line is cut in the same way, though it has little more of a curve to it. Cut up...

and make the return with a slight swell in the center. Lines that are absolutely parallel are lifeless. The swell adds dimensionality even to a simple cut like this.

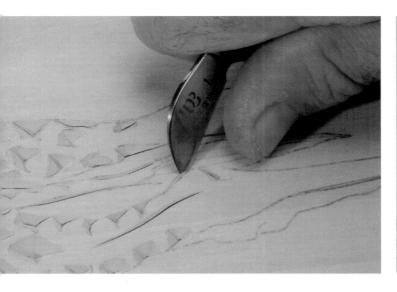

A line above the back of the knee sets the shape of the leg between these last spots, but don't cut all the way to the spots. Let the eye finish the line.

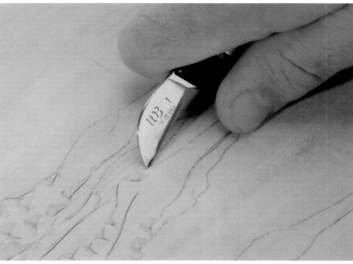

Start just below the spot at the knee and cut the line of the lower leg.

Again on the return of this flat s-curve, swell the cut in the middle.

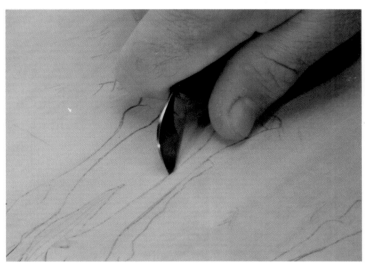

The cut is not too deep on this line.

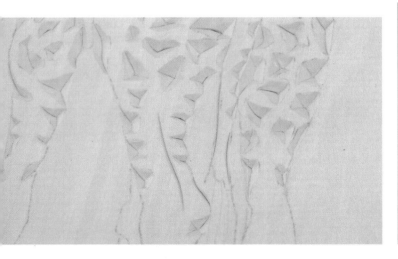

Progress. You can see how the last line carries the eye around the knee.

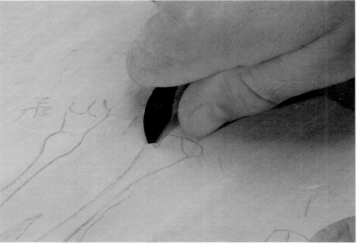

Straighten the knife a little to make the turn at the dew claw. Stop before you reach the hoof.

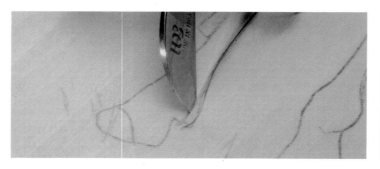

Start the return where you left off. Begin with a rather broad cut at the dew claw.

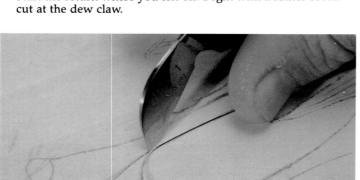

Reduce the width of the cut at the narrow part of the leg...

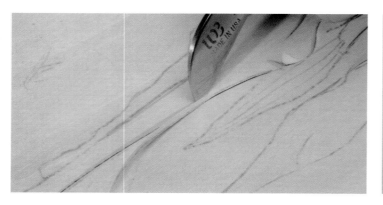

Getting wider as you approach the knee.

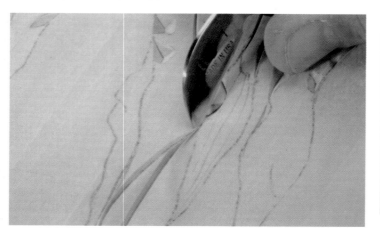

Taper your way out of the cut at the end.

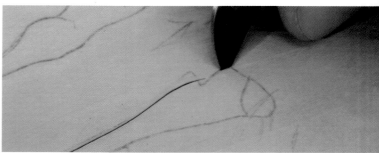

A small line at the back of the hoof suggests its shape. It should not be connected to the line of the leg you just carved.

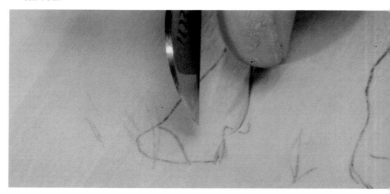

Make the return.

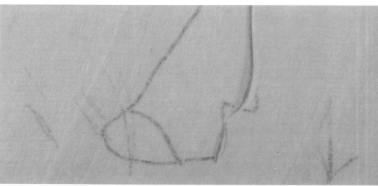

The result. You can see that, while the pattern is a guide, I am not enslaved to copying it exactly. Fewer lines often will tell the story.

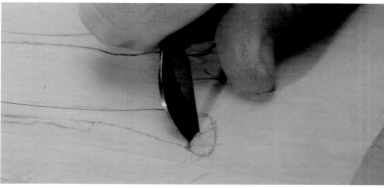

The hoof is formed with three cuts. The first goes pretty deep...

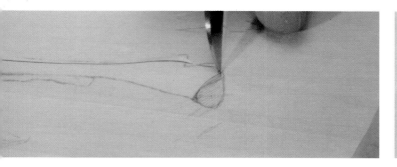

and extends at the end toward the previous cut at the back of the hoof. They do not touch.

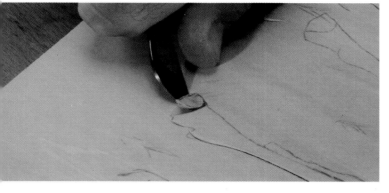

The second cut is along the bottom of the hoof.

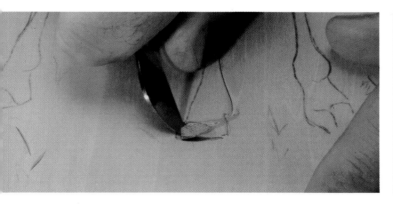

The final cut has a little outward curve to it.

Before continuing erase any overdrawn lines so you can see more clearly. This line was making the hoof look rounder than it was.

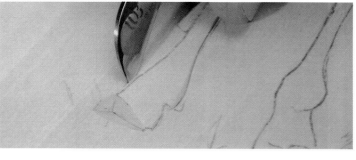

Begin the line of the front of the leg by aligning the blade with the cut of the hoof. You can see this takes me slightly outside of my pencil line.

Follow the line with gentle curves.

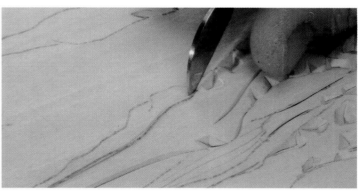

End the cut without touching the spot on the front of the leg.

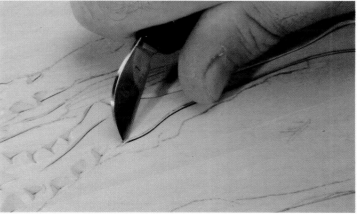

The return will finish the leg.

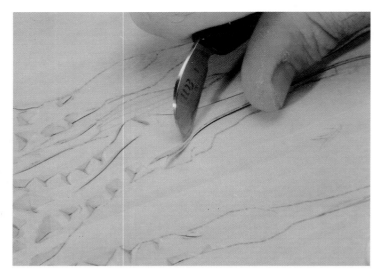

The line should be heavy at the joint...

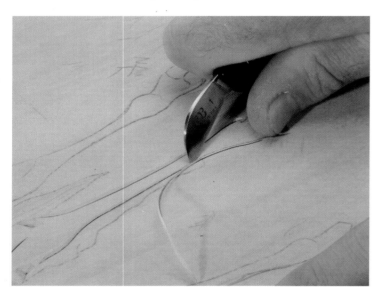

narrow where the leg is narrow...

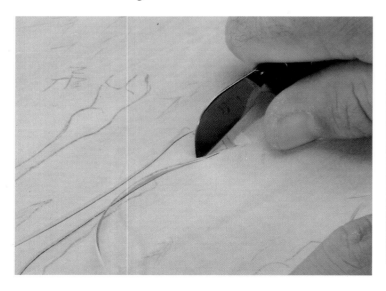

and widen out again at the ankle.

The tail is four adjacent long cuts, with one being separated by the knee, where the tail goes behind it.

Start the first segment where it is adjacent to the knee, cutting away from the previous cut and creating a ridge.

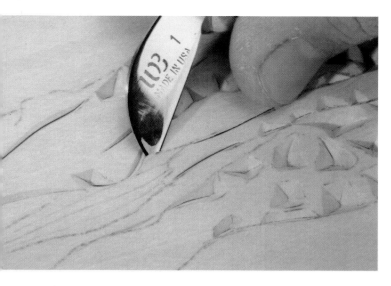

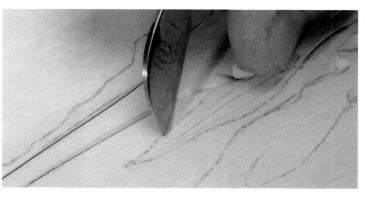

The lower portion of that segment starts about here...

Continue up the tail, stopping before you reach the end of the edge line.

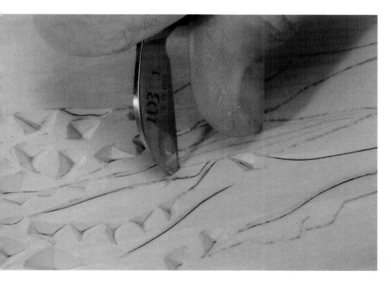

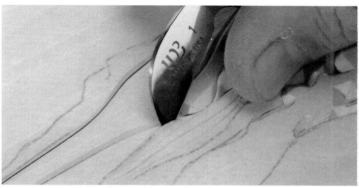

and curves to form a ridge with the adjacent spot at the knee.

The next cut is a counterclockwise rotation at the top...

The return starts quite gently until you get away from the knee.

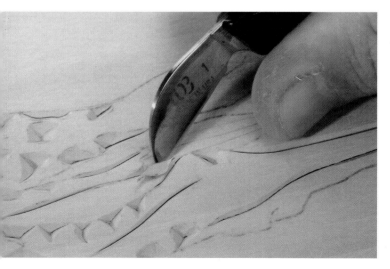

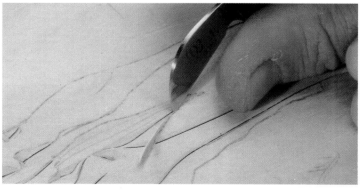

and the chip is completed with a straight cut back to where we started.

Taper the knife out of the wood.

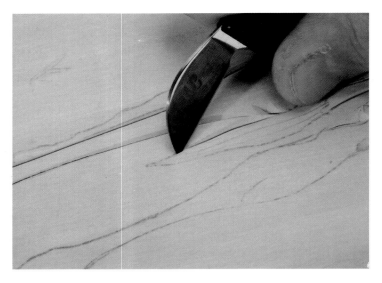

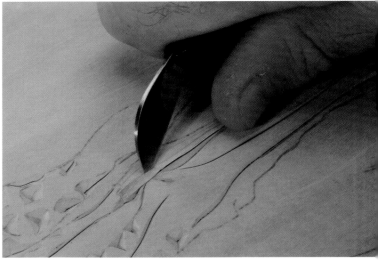

Start the next segment a little lower than the first...

then cut the return. This cut is going in the direction of the grain, and it can be difficult to control the knife so it cuts in the direction I want. I find I get more control by lowering the angle of the knife in this situation.

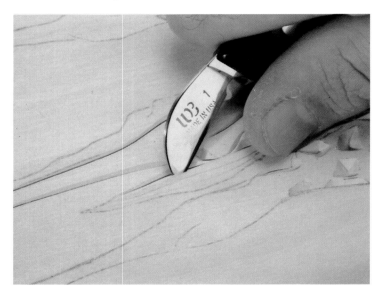

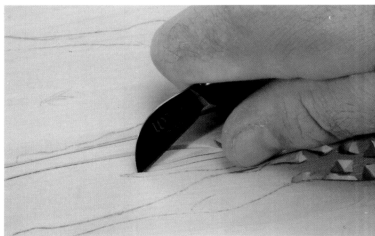

and carve the adjacent side.

Do the third segment in the same way, starting up along the adjacent segment.

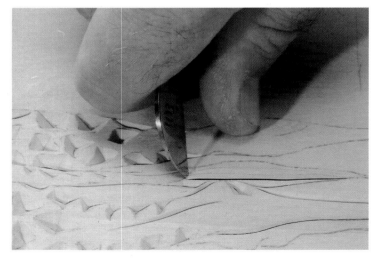

Make a small counterclockwise turn at the top to form a stop...

Instead of a stop at the top of this segment, I simply make the return with a little angle at the start. Again, notice how I have lowered the angle of the blade for going with the grain.

The final segment starts even further down...

The return cut completes it.

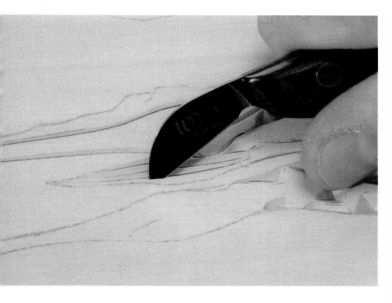

and follows the adjacent ridge.

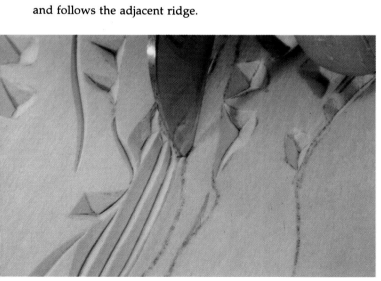

The short stop cut at the top of this segment heads back up the tail.

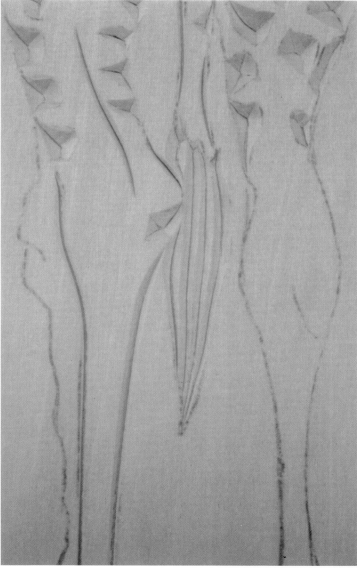

The end of the tail is finished.

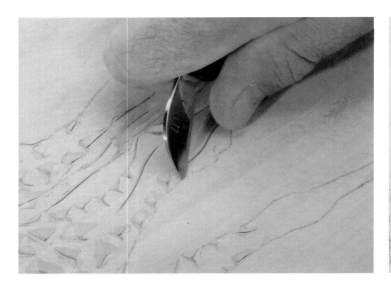

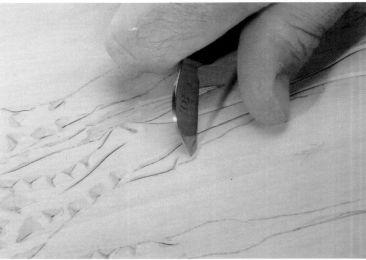

Working away from the back leg I've already carved, I start carving the partially hidden front leg here...

The rest of this leg is one curving cut...

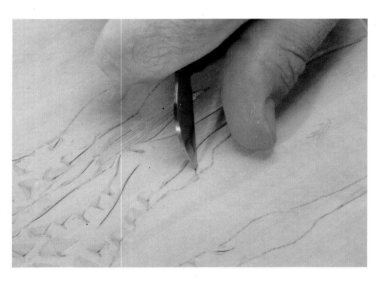

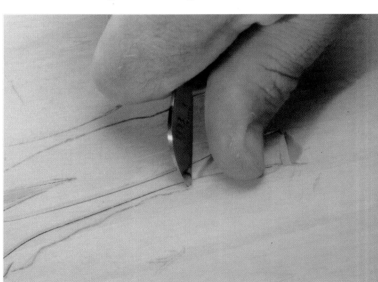

and go to the end of the large knuckle.

turning in at the bottom to suggest the hoof. One thing to keep in mind while carving legs is that the lines need to be strong enough so they look in proportion with the heaviness of the carved body. Two light and the giraffe will take on an impossible look.

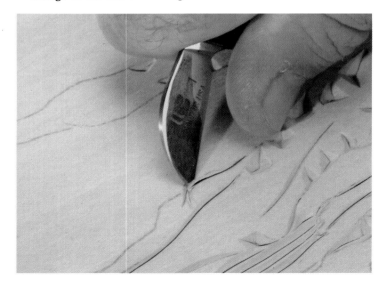

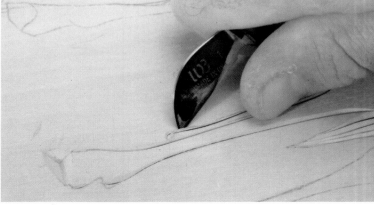

Make the return to establish the gentle curves.

Make the return starting heavy at the bottom...

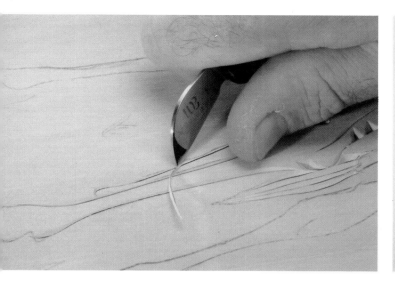

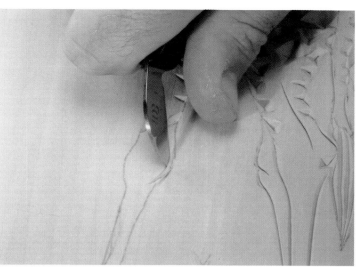

and thin where the leg is thin. I definitely don't want this line to be thicker than the line of the back leg, which is closer.

Cut the return, getting wider in the middle of the cut.

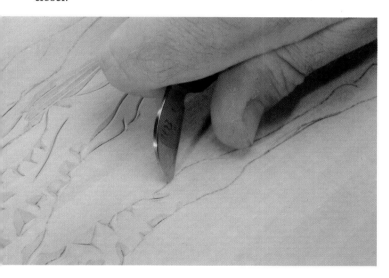

The exposed front leg is much like the back leg we carved earlier. Start at the back of the knee.

Start the second cut below the first cut, not touching...

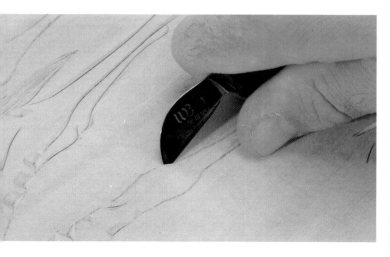

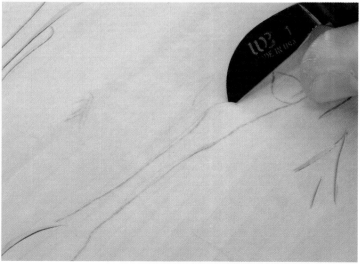

The first cut ends at the bottom of the knee. The curve here is wide so I don't need to stand the blade up very much.

and continue down to the dew claw with one stroke.

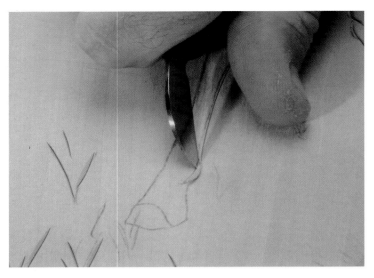

Start the return slightly wide...

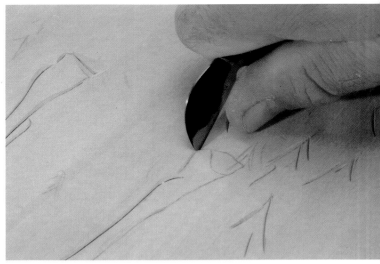

Cut the back edge of the hoof, standing the blade up to make the turn. This should be cut just enough to suggest the turn.

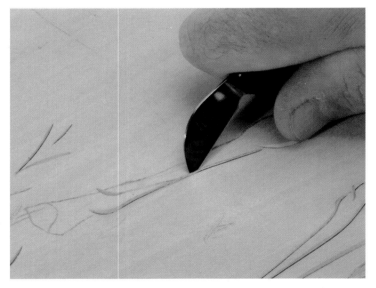

get narrow as you go up the leg...

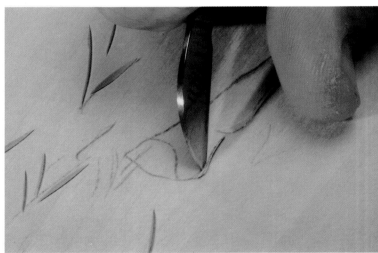

Cut the return as a flat s-curve.

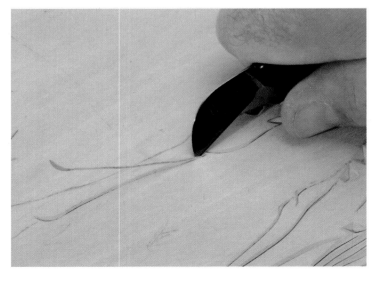

and flare it out just a little as you near the end of the cut.

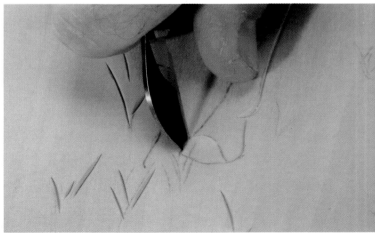

When cutting with the grain, it is most likely to tear when it is the last cut. On this hoof I have a choice, so I'll carve the side that goes with the grain first.

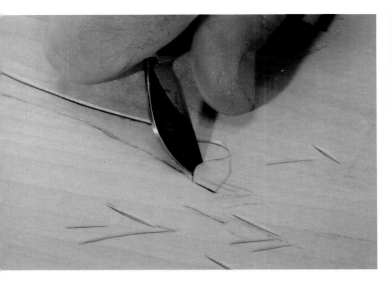

Make the second cut...

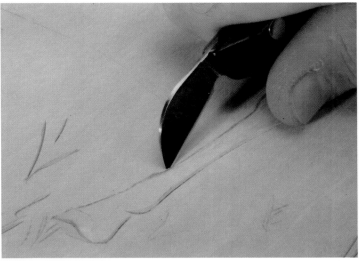

and cut up the leg.

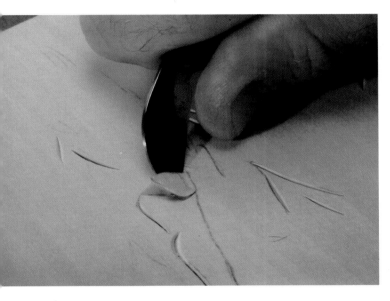

and the third to complete the chip.

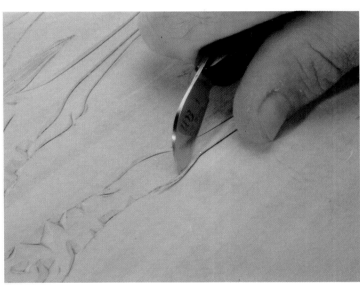

Start the return with a swelled cut...

Align the cut with the front edge of the hoof...

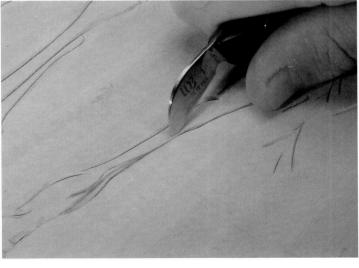

narrowing as you progress down the leg.

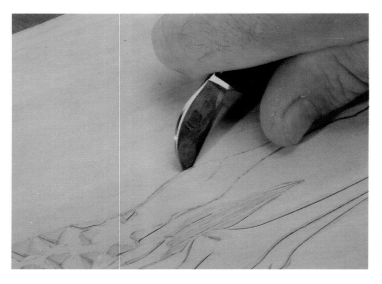

The last leg, the right hind leg, begins with the long outside edge.

A short flat s-curve forms the back of the foot.

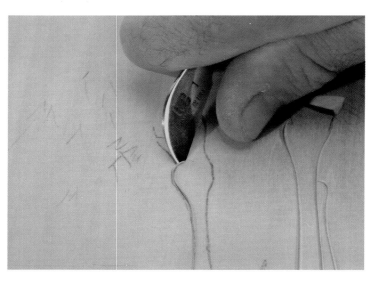

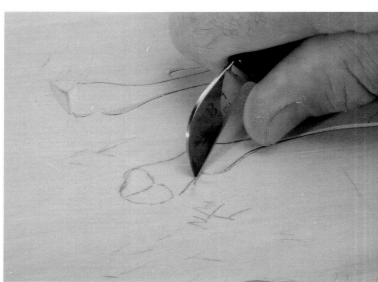

Make one cut all the way to the ankle, slipping the blade out to make a turn that suggests the shape of the ankle.

Make the return.

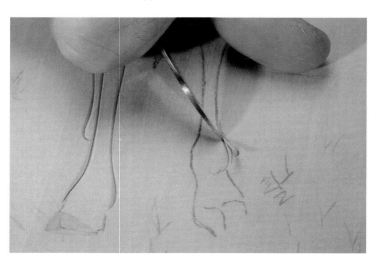

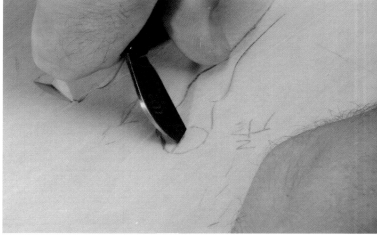

Make the return, swelling slightly at the joint and narrowing as you progress up the leg.

The cloven hoof is visible here at the bottom. It is made up of two curved adjacent triangles. Start along the cleavage with one triangle.

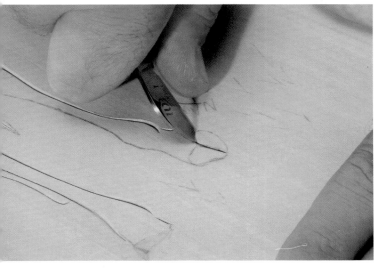

Cut the curved side at the heel...

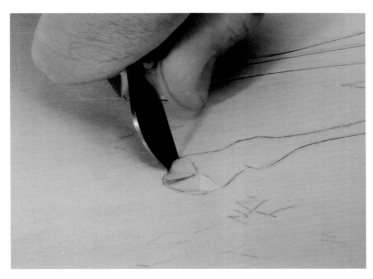

Come up the long curved side...

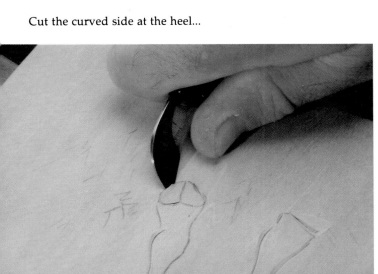

and cut the last curved side, standing the blade up to make a smooth curve.

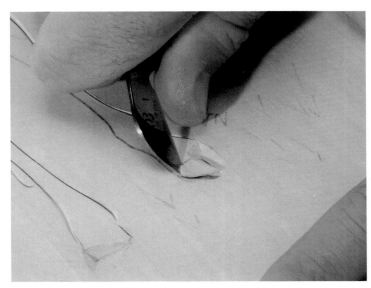

and finish it up on the curved heel side.

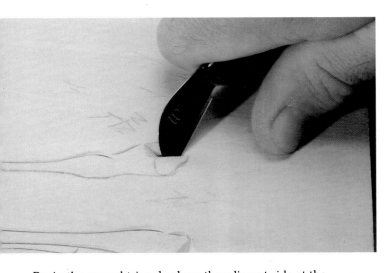

Begin the second triangle along the adjacent side at the middle.

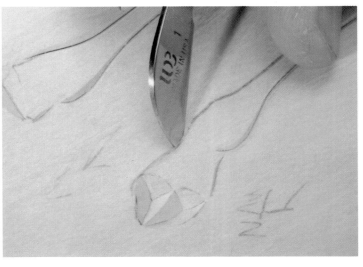

Align the knife with the carved hoof and carve the inside line of the leg with one stroke.

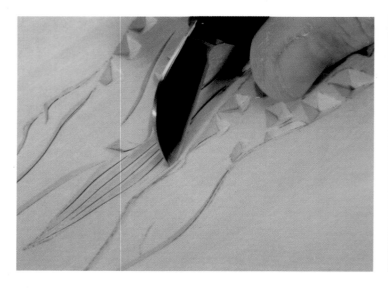

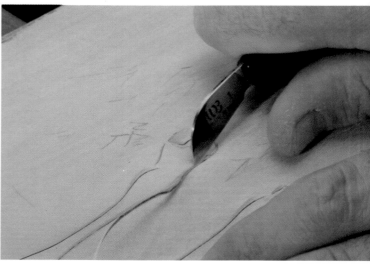

The end of the line should align with, but not touch the edge of the first spot on the leg.

and swelled again at the end.

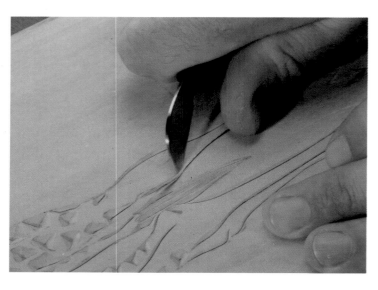

The return line is swelled at the beginning...

The contour of the joint is suggested by this crescent cut at the knee...

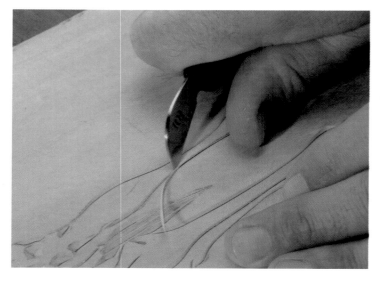

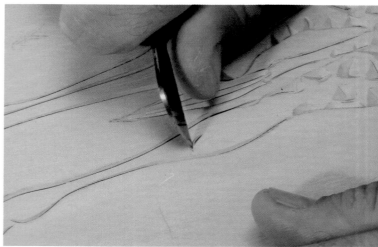

thin in the middle...

and its return.

Finish the carving of the giraffe.

A few blades of grass suggests the ground on which the giraffe stands and keeps him from floating in air. They are made up of simple two-side strokes.

The lines should be slightly curved, not straight.

Cut the return with a slight swell in the middle. The cuts are all shallow.

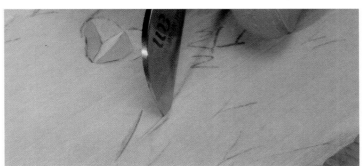

A second or third blade can be added, but they should not touch each other. Cut away from the previously cut blade...

and make the return.

Tree branches enter the design from the sides. I want them to appear natural in form and flow, and I usually like to have them reappear from a clump of leaves. I do not carry the branch all the way to the edge of the board. This keeps the strength of the board intact, and will be covered by a picture frame in any case.

A stop cut cleans up the chip.

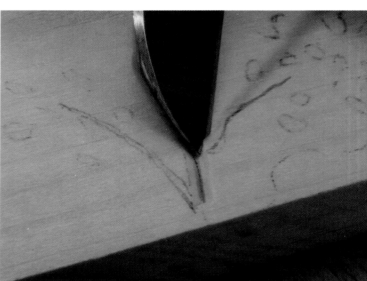

Carve the main section of the branch first. The line here makes more abrupt turns than the legs and is segmented from node to node.

The branches that come off the main branch will be carved to intersect into it. I must be careful not to overcut. If the radiating branch is in line with the direction of the grain, the cut should start in the main branch and go out to the tip of the smaller branch. This prevents breakage.

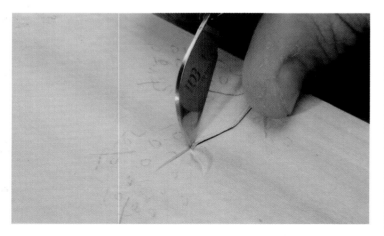

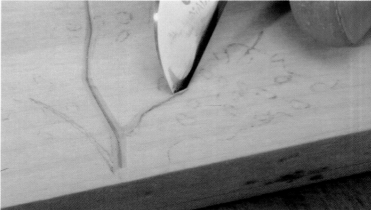

Start at the point and make the return. The branch is still thick here, so I can make a thick cut.

Cut to the end of the branch segment.

Make the return, turning for the quick jog.

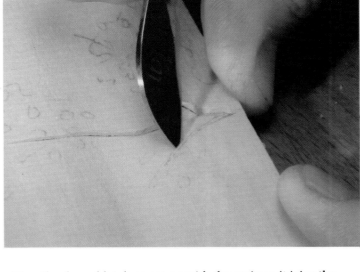

The other branchlet does not go with the grain as it joins the main branch, so I can start at the end, working away from the previous cut.

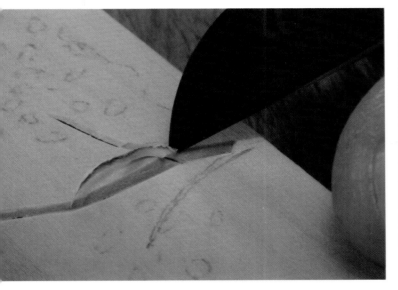

As I approach the main branch the first cut acts as a stop to keep me from shearing off more wood than I want.

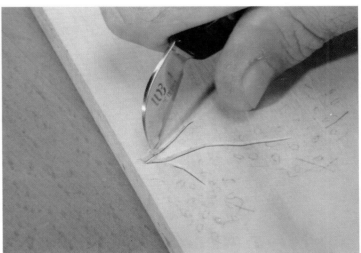

Make the return.

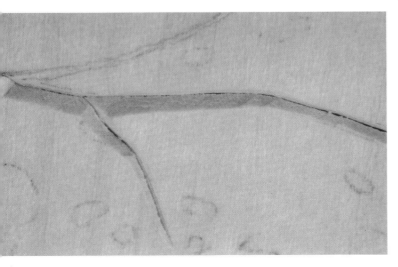

The result.

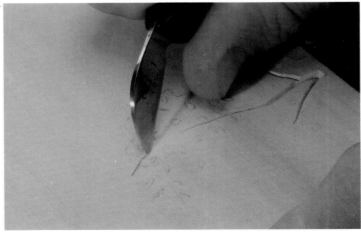

A simple two stroke cut finishes the branches where they re-emerge from the foliage. The cut is similar to what we did on the branch, but more angular than curved to denote the branch nodes. Cut one way...

118193432

and make the return.

and shallow at the end.

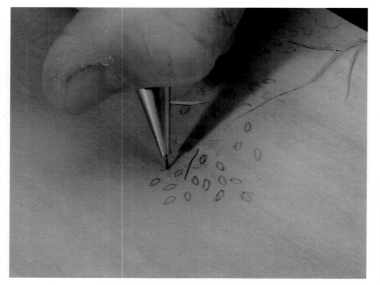

I used two types of leaves in this carving. The larger are pointed ovoids. They should be drawn with random direction and spaces. Do not fill every space with leaves. Instead do the least amount necessary to make the suggestion of foliage.

The return cut is the same.

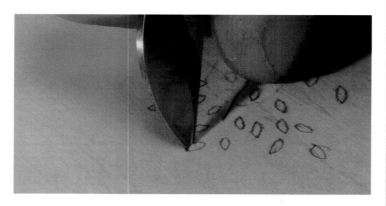

To carve these I choke up a little on the knife so the blade is standing up slightly. The stroke is a simple two cut, starting shallow, going deeper in the middle...

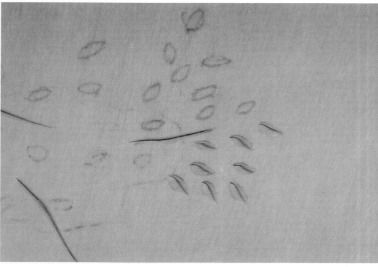

The result.

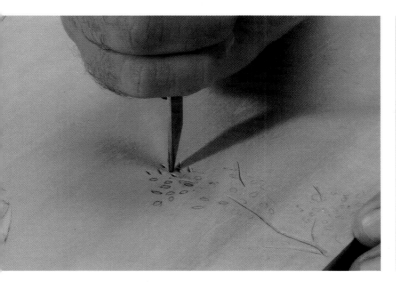

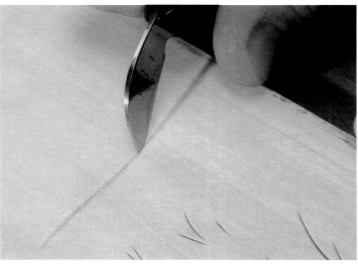

The second leaf is formed with a stab cut. This creates a small triangular leaf that, because of its size, gives the feeling of distance. When mixed with the first type of leaf, as here, it adds depth to the foliage. Simply push the point of the stab knife slightly into the wood. This forces the fibers apart and compressed them.

A simple graceful line creates the suggestion of a horizon .

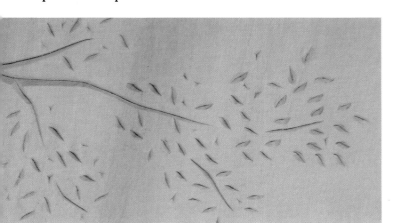

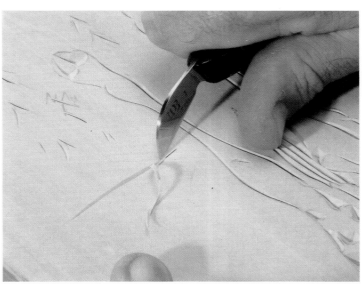

The result of mixing the two cuts.

Make the return, going thicker in the middle and the carving is complete.

Sometimes stab cut leaves can be used on their own, giving the sense of distance to the whole tree, as in this one on the horizon.

A final cleanup is done with an eraser and a gentle touch up with 400 grit sandpaper. Be sure to use a sanding block to avoid softening the sharp lines. The leading edge of the sandpaper should be one that is folded up around the block.

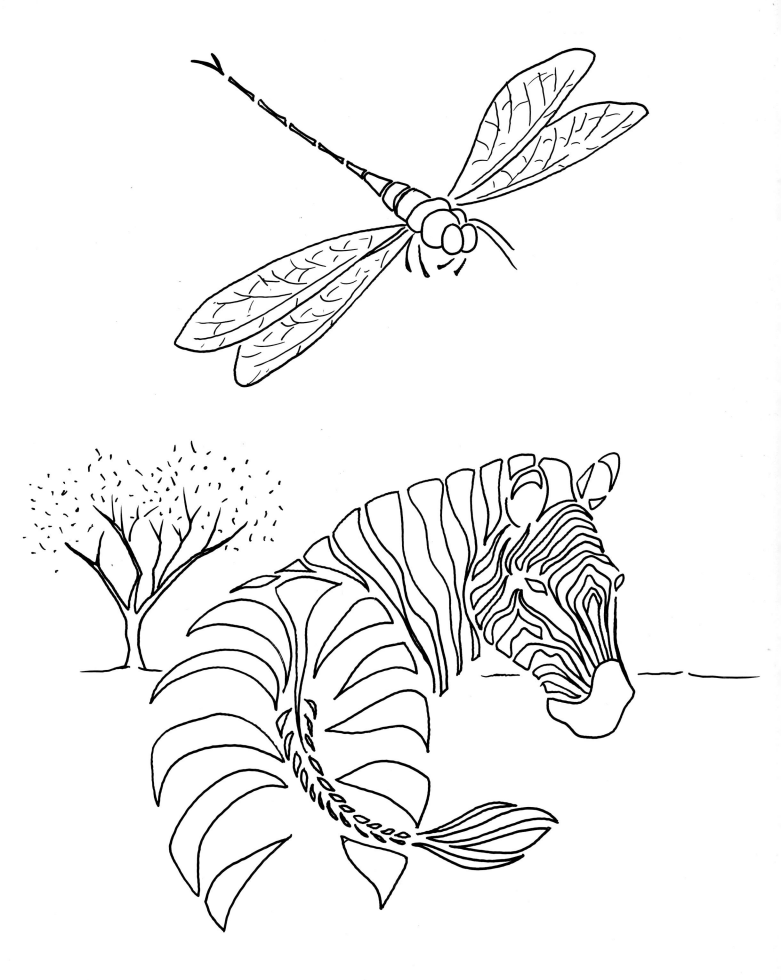